70 Smoothie Rec
Detoxing an

Sara Banks

Table of contents

Introduction

The modern world is plagued with obesity, diabetes and heart disease. At the root of every healthy diet is good abundant, quality fruit and vegetables, yet it can be so difficult to squeeze them into a busy daily schedule. In this short guide, we'll look at 70 fun and easy smoothie and juice recipes that will help your body detox, lose weight and access hidden vibrancy and energy.

Let's go!

Sara Banks

The cleansing, health and weight loss benefits of juices and smoothies

What's so great about smoothies and juices? Everything!

By now, most people know that depleted soils, intensive factory farming methods and pollution work together to undermine the vitamin content of the fruits and vegetables we eat. Though 5 servings a day is great, more is always better – but it can be hard to achieve. With smoothies and juices, you get the concentrated essence of a large amount of fruits and vegetables all in one go.

Smoothies and juices are quick and easy to make, and easy on your digestion – by breaking down or removing the fiber entirely, you provide your body a source of nutrition that absorbs directly, without any strain on your GI tract. This gives your body a much needed break and the chance to cleanse and detoxify itself. Plus, they're delicious!

Add smoothies and juices to your daily life and you'll notice better mood, improved sleep, gorgeous skin, hair and nails, more energy, a strengthened immune system, weight loss and a way to break out of cravings for sugar or bad fats. What's more, kids love smoothies, and you'll soon find hundreds of ways to creatively make your own special and healing blends for you or your entire family.

Before you start juicing

Though it's incredibly easy to make healthy and delicious juices at home in very little time, it doesn't mean that you can just dump your veggies into the machine and hope for the best. Here are a few tips and tricks to make sure you're getting the most out of your juicing routine.

- Generally, juices are best taken on an empty stomach so that the body is able to absorb the nutrients without interference from other food. This could lead to heartburn, indigestion or a feeling of being very full.
- Try not to load up your juices with too many sugary fruits – bananas, apples, pineapples etc. should be added to sweeten things up, but if you're regularly consuming juices made mostly of sweet fruits, you might risk damaging your blood sugar levels, gaining weight and missing out on the more nutritious vegetable ingredients you could opt for instead.
- Make sure that your juicer is super clean at all times. For obvious health reasons, you'll want to make sure that your juicer/blender is clean – rinse it out immediately after use and let it dry in a way that won't let water collect anywhere and leave stains/smells.
- If you make a juice or smoothie and keep it for too long, it'll start to degrade and lose its essence – rather drink it immediately.
- If you decide to undertake a juice cleanse, consult your doctor beforehand, especially if you've experienced any health issues in the past. Juices are not adequate meal replacements and shouldn't be taken in lieu of food for the long term.

Juicing FAQ

Do I have to peel my fruits and vegetables?

If your produce is organic or you grew it yourself, the answer is no. In fact, the peel often contains plenty of fiber and is a great addition to juices and smoothies. Be more wary if they're not organic – wash very thoroughly or just peel. Citrus peels, seeds and pips should all be removed.

Is a blender the same as a juicer?

Nope. The point of juicing is to remove the fibre from the juice and provide nourishment directly to your body without the stress of having to process it as you would whole foods. A blender fails to do this and, although very useful in the kitchen, a blender is not as good as a juicer for the recipes below. You will be unable to process harder vegetables and fruits with a blender.

Do I have to juice the ingredients in any particular order?

Some juice recipes make a point of mentioning how to combine your ingredients, but to be honest, with a good juicer this shouldn't make much of a difference. It's a good idea to add coconut products at the end though, just to combine.

How do I do a juice cleanse/fast?

The answer is: carefully. Unfortunately, the benefits of juicing have occasionally been overblown, with people promoting long periods of drinking nothing but juice. While this may result in temporary weight loss (most often just water), it is not in general a healthy approach.

More than 2 or 3 days of drinking juice alone is likely excessive and without much benefit anyway. Though there is some fat and protein content in some of the recipes below, you will inevitably feel tired and drained after a few days if you don't also eat whole and healthy foods.

Ultimately, it's better to think of juicing as something to supplement an already healthy diet as opposed to something to replace it. Regularly taking in nourishment that doesn't tax the digestive system supports your body's natural healing and detoxifying powers. But it's important to remember that juices in and of themselves contain no special powers. Rather, juicing is a method of obtaining the most from fruits and vegetables.

Many people find that a rich, raw smoothie is the best way to kick off the day, or they eat light, small meals and use smoothies and drinks as snacks throughout the day. Others use them as post or pre-workout supplements. Either way, including more fresh plants in your diet will result in better health, weight loss and a strong, revitalized body. There is no need to shun other foods at all.

If you really do feel like a detox/fast, a good thing to do is start simply with one day. Stop eating early in the evening the day before and on waking, have a glass of warmish water with the juice of 1 lemon to refresh and "wake up" your system. Then, drink juices throughout the day whenever you feel hungry (focus on the veggies more and the fruits less), also including plenty of water and tea to stay hydrated.

If you succeed with this, attempt a three day fast. Choose a variety of juices and smoothies and pay attention to your blood sugar levels and mood. A light laxative tea made of senna leaves can ease any constipation. If hunger pangs get out of hand, a tablespoon of coconut oil will kill them instantly and give you some much needed and easily-digestible fatty acids. Only commit to a longer fast under the supervision of a trained medical practitioner.

Do my fruits and vegetables always need to be raw?

In the raw food community, plants that have not been heated or excessively processed are believed to contain more nutrition than their cooked counterparts. But in some case, cooking certain fruits and vegetables actually makes it *easier* for our bodies to digest and consequently release more nutrition from them.

Raw vs cooked is always a bit of a balancing act. With juicing, one of the aims is to reduce digestive strain on the body. Many raw foodists would hate to admit it, but excessive fiber in the diet from uncooked veggies can be hell on the system. The truth is that mankind has had quite a while to evolve to manage raw and cooked foods.

Some foods are toxic unless cooked properly (potatoes, for example) and others are best fresh (leafy greens). Some are half and half (carrots are best slightly cooked, i.e. steamed).

Moderation is the key. If you are going from a predominantly cooked, processed diet to one with loads and loads of plants, you are going to need time to adapt. Jumping in and eating more veggies I one morning than you previously would in a week is going to be hard on your system. You may experience bloating, gas indigestion and poor absorption.

With juicing, more is not necessarily better. Start slow, include cooked or even frozen veggies if that's what you have, and listen to your body. There is a common mindset that if one green smoothie is good for you, five of them must be five times as good. This is silly. After a certain point, you don't benefit from eating huge amounts of concentrated plant materials – find your balance and stick with something healthful and reasonable.

What do I do with all this pulp I have left over?

Anything you like. Throw on your compost heap, use it make soups and stews or just put it right back into your juice.

Remember that if there are any toxins or pesticides, they'll be concentrated in the skin, so be careful.

Why do I feel terrible drinking juices?

People will say that you are experiencing detox symptoms, but this is usually not the case. More likely is that by juicing, you have removed things from your diet that were addictive or harmful. Caffeine, chocolate, lots of sugar, bad fats, processed foods and the like can leave you feeling awful if you suddenly remove them from your diet.

Eating healthy foods and plenty of water should not leave you feeling bad, and there is not usually any "toxic build up" that you have to suffer through. Your body is effective at eliminating waste *all the time*, whether you have a healthy lifestyle or not. The only problem is that if your lifestyle was less than healthy, suddenly making it more healthy might cause a bit of a shock as you adapt.

Feeling hungry, having slightly bad breath and feeling a bit tired are all normal. Take a closer look if you're fainting, vomiting, experiencing bad diarrhea or feeling extremely ill. You may need to dial it back and go a little more slowly.

What about wheatgrass juice?

Wheatgrass juice is made from tiny sprouted wheat plants and is rich in chlorophyll, amino acids, vitamins and minerals. You can grow wheatgrass at home in small trays and after a few days, when the leaves split, you can harvest them and juice them yourself in a special wheatgrass juicer. Most people advise against using a regular juicer to extract wheatgrass juice. Luckily, it's possible to buy dehydrated or powdered wheatgrass and simply add it to your smoothies and juices that way.

Green juices

Classic green juice

Ingredients

1 small Granny Smith apple
¼ English cucumber or 1 small Israeli cucumber
1 small bunch of kale
1 handful green grapes

This juice is full of iron and vitamin K – just the thing for drinking before your menstrual cycle.

Classic green juice 2

Ingredients

1 ½ cups of shredded kale
2 ribs of celery with a few leaves
1 orange
½ cup chopped parsley
¼ cup chopped mint
1 cup fresh or frozen mango

Classic green juice 3

Ingredients

½ avocado
½ cucumber
½ lemon (peeled)
½ pear (any kind)
½ cup loosely packed cilantro

Small nub of grated ginger
½ cup coconut water
1 tablespoon pea protein powder
Water to thin

Add a shot of protein to your green smoothie by mixing in a tablespoon of pea protein – it's mild in taste and the most beautiful color, plus it's great for vegetarians and fits into most green smoothie recipes.

Super green veggie machine

Ingredients

1 Granny Smith apple
Juice of 1 lemon
1 cucumber (peeled or not, your choice)
4 leaves of red lettuce
¼ cup fresh or frozen mango
1 cup water or ice
1 teaspoon barley grass powder

Look for barley grass powder in health food stores. It's so simple to just throw in a spoon here and there and instantly ups the vitamin and mineral content of any smoothie. Plus, it's so green and lovely!

Vitamin bomb

Ingredients

1 apple – any kind
1 fully ripe pear
1 handful of organic cherries (cherries can be pesticide heavy)
A pinch of cinnamon

This beautiful juice is sweet enough as it is but the cinnamon makes it something special for cooler days or evening.

Avocado "milkshake"

Ingredients

1 large avocado
1 tablespoon honey
½ cup Greek yogurt
1 teaspoon vanilla extract (try avoid the synthetic essence, or even find a whole vanilla pod instead)

It's hard to describe how good this smoothie is to people who are used to having avocado in savory dishes. Avocados are full of all the best kinds of fat and are a healthy way to treat your hair, skin and nails while keeping you sated.

Acne healer

Ingredients

1 cup kefir (coconut, water or milk kefir)
½ cup strong brewed nettle tea
1 Granny Smith apple
1 Tablespoon coconut oil
The juice of 1 lime
A big handful of fresh mint leaves
½ cup parsley – any kind, leaves and stems

This smoothie is a real does of TLC for inflamed and irritable skins. Nettle tea balances disrupted hormones and kefir and mint make sure that your system is cleansed from the inside out.

Chlorophyll smoothie

Ingredients

1 Granny Smith apple

½ cucumber
½ tablespoon honey
1 tablespoon wheatgrass powder or shot of fresh wheatgrass juice

Adjust the honey to counteract the bitterness of the wheatgrass. This is an incredible smoothie to make when you feel the first sniffles of a cold coming on or if you've been feeling a bit under the weather.

The vegetarian's secret

Ingredients

1 ½ cups coconut water
1 big handful of kale or spinach
5 or 6 ribs of celery
The juice of 1 lemon (squeeze directly)
1 cup of chopped parsley

This smoothies is rich in iron, which can sometimes be in short supply in a vegetarian or vegan diet. The parsley is rich in vitamin C and very refreshing. Remember to drink on an empty stomach.

Refreshing pear

Ingredients

1 pear
½ cucumber
3 or 4 big lettuce leaves
1 celery stalk

This is a delicately sweet and almost elegant blend for when you want something light and easy – plus pears are full of fiber and the cucumber and lettuce are incredibly hydrating, making it the perfect drink for healing after a bout of gastroenteritis.

IBS relief

1 ½ cup of unsweetened aloe vera juice (with the chunks)
A handful of peppermint leaves
A very small nub of fresh ginger
1 tablespoon coconut oil
½ teaspoon stevia powder (avoid other artificial sweeteners or honey)

A damaged intestinal lining can make it difficult to digest anything, but this blend is very mild and will help to soothe and calm and inflamed GI tract. The aloe vera can heal small lesions, peppermint reduces symptoms of both constipation and diarrhea and the medium chain fatty acids are excellent in combating bacterial overgrowth and Candida.

Lemon, ginger and apple

Ingredients

The juice of 1 lemon
A small nub of ginger
1 Granny Smith Apple
½ head of lettuce – any kind

This is a beautiful green juice that will lift your spirits on a hot day and fill your body with regenerating plant phenols. If you're feeling adventurous, add a few leaves of fresh basil to the mix.

Matcha blend

Ingredients

1 cup almond or rice milk
1 tablespoon green matcha powder (a kind of whole green tea)
1 tablespoon honey
1 peach

Match is one of the richest sources of antioxidants and very many times more nourishing than regular green tea. The plant phenols in this juice will speed up thermogenesis in your body, making your metabolism more efficient. This makes it a great tool for suppressing hunger and cravings, losing water weight and burning fat.

Quick veggie juice

Ingredients

2 large tomatoes
1 carrot
½ cucumber
1 celery rib
¼ cup chopped parsley
1 cup baby spinach
½ cup ice or crushed ice

Lettuce, jicama and lime

Ingredients

5 or 6 Romaine lettuce leaves
¼ avocado
½ cucumber
½ Granny Smith apple
½ cup chopped jicama
1 whole, squeezed lime
1 medjool date (with pit removed)
4 tablespoons of hemp or pea protein powder
A handful of cilantro leaves

Can you really juice lettuce leaves? Yes, of course! Lettuce and jicama are both incredibly light and refreshing and taste almost like a cocktail when mixed with cilantro and lime. The hemp/pea protein adds a bit of oomph and the date gives it some natural sweetness.

Limeade with cilantro

Ingredients

A few handfuls of spinach or kale (baby spinach is extra nice)
½ cup of fresh cilantro (stalks included)
3 medium bananas
The juice of 1 lime
A small nub of ginger
2 cups of water

This is a very light and refreshing juice and surprisingly good – many people don't think of adding cilantro to smoothies.

Mojito juice

Ingredients

A big bunch of mint leaves and stalks
The juice of two limes
1 orange
1 cup ice or water

This is a light and fun juice that can serve as a base for other veggies you might like to add, or as a refreshing shot during the day. Add a tomato and some spinach for a zingy vegetable juice or else a banana and a cup of pineapple for a more tropical twist.

Red juices

Classic red juice

Ingredients

1 beetroot
1 carrot
1 Granny Smith apple

½ thumb sized nub of ginger

This red juice is deeply satisfying, full of nutrition and very easy on the digestion. It's great for sluggish bowels due to the high fiber content, and will release energy into your bloodstream slowly and steadily. Thin with a little water if it's too thick and be warned – beet juice can turn your urine and feces bright pink/red, so don't be worried if this happens, it's totally normal.

Red cabbage and blueberry smoothie

Ingredients

2 small bananas
1 cup fresh or frozen blueberries
1 tablespoon chia seeds (you can pre-soak them for 15 minutes to soften)
2 cups of shredded red cabbage
1 cup water or crushed ice

If you feel a bit strange putting cabbage into the juicer, don't worry, this smoothie is absolutely delicious. Cabbage is a severely underrated vegetable and when you see its beautiful purple color when combined with the blueberries, you may decide to make it a regular indulgence.

Anti-aging elixir

Ingredients

1 cup of frozen mixed berries (strawberries, cherries, blackberries etc)
½ small papaya
1 tablespoon crushed flaxseeds
½ teaspoon odorless omega 3 oil (look in health food stores)

This juice is rich in skin-pampering anti-oxidants that reduce free radical damage on your tissues, and the omega 3 fatty acids help keep your skin strong, healthy and supple.

Cranberry miracle

Ingredients

1 cup frozen or fresh mixed berries
¼ large avocado
1 tablespoon ground flaxseeds
½ thumb sized nub of ginger
½ cup of ice cubes or crushed ice
2 cup cranberry juice concentrate or 1 cup fresh cranberries if you can find them

Cranberries are strong and tart, but there's nothing better for flushing and supporting the lymphatic system, as well as soothing and healing urinary tract infections. Cranberry juice can be taken as is, but this juice lets you enjoy the healing power of cranberries in a much more delicious way.

Unusual red smoothie

Ingredients

1 tablespoon Dutch process cocoa powder
2 tablespoons hemp seeds
Small pinch of stevia
1/3 cup fresh or frozen cherries
1 cup water or crushed ice
About 5 red endive leaves

When eaten alone, endive can be quite bitter, but here it is paired with the sweetness of the cherries and stevia to create a very balanced and strangely appealing blend. This is the ultimate cold weather smoothie and just the thing when you're feeling bored of the same old carrot/kale combinations.

Blood orange and vanilla

Ingredients

1 peeled blood orange

Tiny dash of vanilla extract
¼ cup crushed ice or ice cubes
¼ cup plain Greek yogurt
2 tablespoons frozen orange juice concentrate

Blood oranges are like the more beautiful cousins of regular oranges. The fresh, earthy flavor is perfectly balanced by the vanilla and mildness of the yogurt, giving you a gorgeous shot of vitamin C.

Berry explosion

Ingredients

I cup coconut milk (or coconut water for a lighter smoothie)
½ cup raspberries
½ cup blackberries
½ cup goji berries (soak for 10 minutes if they are dried)
½ cup strawberries
1 tablespoon coconut oil
1 tablespoon ground flaxseed
2 pitted dates (medjool dates are the juiciest)

Berries of all kinds are natures little antioxidant powerhouses, and this smoothie is full of them. Try it before a stressful exam or when recovering from an illness to give you that little bit extra.

Super veggie juice

Ingredients

2 big, very ripe tomatoes
¼ cup chopped chives
1 red bell pepper
2 celery ribs, leaves included
1 carrot
½ cup ice cubes or crushed ice
A small bit of fresh jalapeno

It's easy to get stuck on kale as the main green juice vegetable, but this juice proves that other veggies can also make a juice that is refreshing, savory and fortifying. In place of the jalapeno, you could even add a dash of Tabasco sauce for a bit of zing.

The fat burner

Ingredients

1 beetroot
3 carrots
2 garlic cloves
A big handful of parsley
1 or 2 radishes
1 tablespoon coconut oil

This feisty little smoothie is more than meets the eye. The cleansing and diuretic properties of these veggies will flatten your belly, flush out toxins and keep you feeling full and nourished while giving your body the chance to burn off excess fat. Add a small serving of protein and you have a complete and very healthy meal.

Classic strawberry and kiwi

Ingredients

1 ½ cups of apple juice or 1 ½ granny smith apples
1 banana
½ cup frozen strawberries
1 teaspoon honey
1 kiwi fruit

High fiber and full of vitamin C and plant phenols, this smoothie is great at warding off colds and flus. Freeze slightly and take with you for sipping on during a gym session to keep you hydrated and refreshed.

Lemon blueberry

Ingredients

1 cup water or ice
¼ up blueberries
Juice of 1 lemon

You don't always need tons of ingredients to make a good juice. If you're feeling fancy, a sprig of mint tops this smoothie nicely, but it's a winner just the way it is.

Chocolate cherry surprise

Ingredients

1 cup frozen or fresh black or red cherries
¼ cup macadamia nut butter
1 tablespoon Dutch process, high quality cocoa powder
1 cup almond or rice milk
½ banana

This creamy, chocolatey smoothie is the smart way to get your cocoa fix. Find good cocoa powder – which is very rich in antioxidants – and combine with very ripe cherries and a bit of macadamia nut butter to add richness and lovely velvet texture. You could also substitute strawberries for cherries.

Raspberry and orange

Ingredients

1 cup orange juice or 1 orange
½ cup plain Greek yogurt
1 cup ice or crushed ice
½ tablespoon honey
1 cup frozen raspberries

Even the fussiest child will drink this smoothie, as it tastes so much like a strawberry milkshake.

Craving killer

Ingredients

1 cup frozen or fresh strawberries
1 cup milk (or substitute soy, almond or rice milk)
1 tablespoon pumpkin seeds
1 teaspoon sunflower seeds
1 tablespoon cold pressed flaxseed oil

The great thing about this smoothie is that it's so sweet and rich – and completely innocent. The flaxseed oil and other seeds give you a healthy shot of hunger-busting omegas and the strawberries are just sweet enough without being too much. The next time you're craving a slice of cake, try this instead – it's almost better.

Watermelon dream

3 cups of chopped watermelon (try remove as many of the seeds as possible)
½ English cucumber
½ cup of chopped curly leaf parsley

This is such a light and elegant juice that you may keep returning to it in the hotter summer months. You could also replace the watermelon with honeydew melon or even papaya, although the watermelon has a lightness and freshness that's very unique. Serve with plenty of ice and you'll have a health tonic that's perfect for healing the cells, calming digestion and rehydrating and cooling the entire body.

Banana, green tea and blueberry

Ingredients

¼ cup water
1 green tea bag
½ tablespoon of honey
1 ½ cups of blueberries, fresh or frozen

½ banana
¾ cup whole milk or coconut milk

First, you'll need to brew the tea in the water. While you let it steep, whizz the other ingredients in the juicer. Then add the tea and whizz again. This makes a great early morning smoothie and will keep you going.

Coconut inspired smoothies

After workout smoothie

Ingredients

1 cup of pure coconut water
1/3 cup of canned litchis (in water is better, in syrup is fine if you work out vigorously)
1 peach

This rich and lovely smoothie is great for after a gym session – the electrolytes in the coconut water and the easily absorbable fruit sugars mean you can rehydrate and recover more quickly.

Blueberry smoothie

Ingredients

1 cup of frozen or fresh blueberries
1 banana
1 cup coconut milk
A pinch of cinnamon
1 tablespoon hemp seeds
1 tablespoon chia seeds
1 tablespoon avocado or olive oil

This smoothie tastes so good you won't believe it's filled with so many healthy things – good fats, vitamins, minerals, phytochemicals and plenty of antioxidants, this smoothie makes a breakfast that's hard to beat.

Kidney detox

Ingredients

½ English cucumber (no need to peel it)
1 cup coconut water
1 tablespoon flax or chia seeds
1 tablespoon honey
1 cup blueberries

This smoothies is hydrating and helps you release excess water weight. The kidneys work hard to detoxify your body, and this smoothie is full of ingredients that support that function.

Christmas smoothie

Ingredients

¾ cup of pumpkin puree
¼ cup coconut water
¼ cup coconut milk
1 tablespoon chia seeds
2 teaspoons ground cinnamon
½ teaspoon nutmeg
½ teaspoon pumpkin pie spice
½ cup ice cubes or crushed ice
1 tablespoon honey

The great thing about this smoothie is that it'll remind you almost exactly of pumpkin pie – it's heavy, rich and delectable, and the cinnamon and spices will warm you in colder weather. Replace the honey with ¼ teaspoon of stevia powder if you're serious about reducing the sugar/glycaemic load – you probably won't even notice the difference.

Coconut and goji

Ingredients

1 cup coconut milk
1 frozen banana
½ cup frozen strawberries
½ cup goji berries

Goji berries are also called wolfberries and are extremely high in antioxidants. Make sure you juice them well to avoid any gritty pieces.

Coconut-peanut butter swirl

Ingredients

2 tablespoons smooth, sugar free peanut butter
½ cup coconut milk or cream
½ cup ice cubes or crushed ice
2 medium bananas
1 tablespoon coconut oil

Sometimes you just don't feel like a traditional smoothie. This smoothie is quite an indulgence, but is full of plant sugars and good fats to nourish you after a hard workout or when you're feeling hungrier than usual. Add a tiny pinch of salt to bring out the best in the peanut butter. This smoothie can be used as a light lunch or when you're on the go and don't have time to prepare something more elaborate. Try experimenting with macadamia nut butter, almond nut butter or even tahini (sesame seed paste). A tablespoon of honey can be added in this case.

Cinnamon blood sugar balancer

Ingredients

2 teaspoons ground cinnamon
1 cup coconut milk
1 pear (Asian pears are best if you can find one)
1 small Granny Smith apple

Cinnamon lowers the glycaemic index of other foods and has a stabilizing effect on blood sugar levels. A great smoothie to drink when you feel hunger pangs/lightheadedness is getting the better of you.

Smooth watermelon and kiwi

Ingredients

1 cup coconut milk – best if you can semi freeze it first
3 kiwis
2 cups watermelon

You could easily change this recipe around by using other kinds of melon in place of the watermelon. Amazing served extra chilled on a hot day.

Orange Juices

Vitamin C juice

Ingredients

1 grapefruit – any kind
1 orange
2 peeled kiwi fruits, yellow or green
1 teaspoon rosehip syrup

Rosehip syrup has the highest concentration of vitamin C of any other plant, and when combined with these other vitamin C powerhouses, will give your body a boost.

Savory carrot smoothie

Ingredients

5 or 6 carrots
3 tomatoes
2 red bell peppers
1 cup watercress
1 cup baby spinach
1 seeded jalapeno pepper (optional)
4 stalks celery
4 cloves of garlic

Not every smoothie has to be sweet. This elegant carrot smoothie is spicy, rich and packed full of veggies that will boost your immune system and give you a kick of energy to combat that early afternoon slump. If you love Bloody Marys you'll love this carrot smoothie.

Cape gooseberry

Ingredients

¼ cup yogurt or kefir
½ banana
4 or 5 strawberries
A small handful of cape gooseberries (around 10)
1 medjool date
1 teaspoon lemon juice
¼ cup of crushed ice

Gooseberries can be a little tart for most people, but when blended with strawberries and dates in this lovely smoothie, all is forgiven. Super rich in antioxidants and excellent for the skin.

Honeydew and vanilla

½ honeydew melon
¼ scraped vanilla bean pod (if you can't find one, just use ½ teaspoon vanilla extract)
1 tablespoon honey
½ cucumber

This smoothie is like heaven in a glass. Honeydew is low in fat and calories but rich in fiber, vitamins and minerals. Balanced with a little cucumber, you'll feel like an angel after a sip.

Serious protein smoothie

Ingredients

½ cup cooked sweet potato pulp
¼ cup chopped or slivered almonds
1 orange
1 apple, any kind

This is excellent workout food and very nourishing for your body after intense exercise. It's full of protein and electrolytes for muscle repair and rehydration.

Basic carrot and apple

1 small apple
5 carrots
A tiny nub of ginger

This classic is a great way to get beta carotene in your diet as well as encourage your body to release retained water.

Morning grapefruit zinger

Ingredients

2 grapefruits
Pinch of cinnamon
½ cup coconut water

This looks like a simple recipe but a glass of this grapefruit elixir in the morning will pep you up way more than coffee. The cinnamon is warming and energizing and the grapefruit cleanses and flushes the digestive system.

Acai smoothie

½ cup acai juice
½ cup frozen mango
½ cup chopped jicama
1 cup ice or crushed ice

This is a great smoothie to sip throughout the day and is incredibly low in fat and calories, yet high in vitamin C.

Summer juice

1 grapefruit
The juice of 1 lime or lemon
1 cup of strong brewed hibiscus flowers (remove the actual petals)
½ cup pineapple

1 tablespoon coconut oil
½ cup coconut water
1 banana
A few sprigs of mint
A little ice

This is very refreshing and cooling and just the thing to put in a tiny paper umbrella and enjoy next to the pool. Adjust the amount of ice to thicken or thin as desired.

Island dream

1 chopped mango
2 tablespoons barley green powder (look in a health food store)
1 tablespoon coconut oil
1 cup water/ice
A few sprigs of mint
A handful of red or green grapes

This is an unusual but almost addictive blend of nutrient rich frutis. You could add a teaspoon of honey for sweetness but this smoothie tends to be just sweet enough without going over the top.

Protein peach

Ingredients

1 cup milk (substitute soy, rice or almond milk if desired)
½ cup frozen or fresh peaches
¼ cup Greek yogurt
A pinch of powdered ginger
1 tablespoon whey or protein powder
¼ cup ice cubes or crushed ice
½ cup strawberries, fresh or frozen

Juice/blend everything together for a smoothie with a lot of body – just the thing for before or after a long workout or when you're not hungry enough for a full meal.

Pineapple cream

1 cup plain Greek yogurt
1 cup pineapple chunks, fresh or frozen
½ small avocado
½ cup water

Pineapple contains bromelain and other healthy enzymes and phytochemicals. The pulp left over from this smoothie makes and incredible exfoliating mask. Alternatively, freeze this smoothie for a while and you'll have a delicious frozen dessert. Top with whipped coconut cream or fresh berries.

Golden antioxidant smoothie

1 cup pineapple, fresh or frozen
A small nub of ginger
1 teaspoon ground turmeric
1 banana

Turmeric is one of the best spices to have in your pantry, and is full of antioxidants. This smoothie takes the strong earthy flavor of turmeric and balances it with its botanical cousin ginger and the sweetness of pineapple.

Papaya princess

Ingredients

1 whole papaya
½ cup pineapple chunks (use fresh but canned is OK in a pinch)
1 cup plain Greek yogurt
1 teaspoon coconut extract
1 teaspoon coconut oil
1 teaspoon ground flaxseeds (soak first for 15 minutes to soften)

This is the kind of smoothie that you'll want to decorate. Halve a pineapple slice and cut a slit down the middle to hang on the side of a tall, pretty glass and add a fun curly straw for a tropical treat that tastes amazing and is full of vitamins and minerals.

Apricot and mango

Ingredients

6 apricots without pits
1 cup Greek yogurt
2 very ripe mangoes
¼ teaspoon vanilla extract
1 cup of ice cubes or crushed ice
1 ½ tablespoons lemon juice

Serve with a few lemon peel twirls as garnish.

Raspberry detox

Ingredients

1 cup fresh or frozen raspberries
1 cup almond milk
1 tablespoon honey
A small grated nub of ginger
1 teaspoon ground flaxseed (or a teaspoon flaxseed oil)
2 teaspoons fresh lemon juice

Fruit salad

Ingredients

½ cup frozen or fresh berries
½ cup pineapple
½ banana
½ orange or ½ cup orange juice
½ cup plain Greek yogurt

This recipe is great for when you have a few bits and pieces left over from other smoothie recipes. Don't worry if you occasionally use store bought orange juice – just make sure it's the best quality you can find, i.e organic, with pulp and not made from concentrate.

Other juices and smoothies

Simple smoothie

Ingredients

1 cup of any of the above juices, or even store-bought
1 cup ice cubes or crushed ice
1 peeled banana
½ cup Greek yogurt

Depending on the kind of juice you use, you might like to experiment with a naturally flavored yogurt to complement it.

Blackberry-cinnamon treat

Ingredients

1 cup fresh or frozen blackberries
1 cup almond milk
1 tablespoon flax seeds
A pinch of cinnamon
A few big spinach leaves
1 teaspoon vanilla extract
1 tablespoon raw honey

This is a well-balanced and delicious smoothie that tastes like dessert and is full of goodness. You might try freezing this blend to make yummy popsicles.

Detox blend

Ingredients

3 carrots

3 ribs of celery (with or without the leaves)
2 small Israeli cucumbers
½ bunch of kale or spinach
½ bunch of curly leaf parsley
½ bunch cilantro
The juice of one lemon
1 cup of brewed stinging nettle tea

This is a very interesting and incredibly healthy juice that will support your body in detoxing. If you're not a fan of green juices, this one makes a nice compromise with plenty of sweet carrots.

Almond chai

1 cup of almond milk
1 tablespoon coconut oil
A pinch of ground cinnamon
A pinch of ground cardamom
1 tablespoon brown sugar or honey
A pinch of nutmeg
A tiny pinch of black pepper
A pinch of ground ginger
1 teaspoon Dutch process cocoa powder
A pinch of ground cloves

Here, "a pinch" is more or less to your own taste, and you can adjust this recipe to suit how spicy you want your chai. Have it room temperature or heat the liquid ingredients in a double boiler before adding the spices for a warm drink.

Banana ginger slush

Ingredients

I medium banana
1 cup vanilla yogurt (or 1 cup plain Greek yogurt with a teaspoon vanilla essence)
1 Tablespoon honey (or 1/8 teaspoon stevia powder)

½ teaspoon grated ginger

This is a great smoothie when you're after something simple, thick and lovely. The ginger and yogurt are great at settling upset stomachs and if you freeze everything, you'll get a nice creamy frozen yogurt style slush.

Black spirulina detox

Ingredients

1 small banana
½ cup blueberries
¼ avocado
1 teaspoon spirulina powder
1 scoop pea protein powder
½ cup almond or coconut milk

The intimidating color of spirulina can be a bit off-putting, but this blue-green algae is one of the earth's richest sources of chlorophyll and is packed with healthy vitamins and minerals. Add a splash of honey if the taste is a bit too mossy.

Hemp, mint and apple

Ingredients

½ Granny smith apple
8 mint leaves (fresh)
5 leaves of lettuce (any kind)
¼ cup frozen berries (any kind)
1 cup water or crushed ice
2 tablespoons hemp hearts

Hemp hearts are shelled hemp seeds and can be bought in health food stores. Together with these other very light and refreshing ingredients, they create a juice that is cleansing and uplifting.

Papaya and kefir

Ingredients

1 cup chopped papaya
1 cup kefir – either milk, water or coconut kefir
Juice from ½ lime
1 tablespoon honey

Drinking kefir is simply the best way to balance intestinal flora, support your natural probiotic balance and soothe all tummy ailments. A daily serving of this papaya and kefir smoothie will "heal and seal" your intestinal lining, boosting your immune system, flattening your tummy and allowing your system to properly absorb nutrition from the food you eat.

Aztec war tonic

Ingredients

1 cup milk (or almond or rice milk)
1 scoop protein powder of your choice (pea, whey, hemp etc.)
1 Tablespoons chia seeds
1 tablespoons coconut oil
1 tablespoon lucuma powder
1 ½ tablespoons cacao nibs (or cocoa powder if you can't find them)
2 tablespoons maca powder

The ingredients in this ancient inspired smoothie are a little hard to come by, but if you can find them you'll be glad you did. Lucuma is a natural sweetener, and the other ingredients were often rationed to Inca and Aztec soldiers to strengthen and ready them for battle. After a cup of this, you can take on whatever your day has to throw at you.

PB and banana

Ingredients

¼ cup smooth, sugar free peanut butter
1 large banana
1 tablespoon cocoa powder
1 cup ice or crushed ice
1 tablespoon honey

Kids will love this rich, sweet smoothie, and you could even switch out the peanut butter with macadamia nut butter or almond nut butter.

Mexican iced coffee

Ingredients

½ cup strong coffee
½ cup almond milk
¼ teaspoon cinnamon
1/8 teaspoon almond extract
3 tablespoons honey

Lemon poppy seed

Ingredients

Juice and zest of ½ lemon
1 cup plain Greek yogurt
2 tablespoons honey
½ cup almond milk
2 teaspoons poppy seeds

Conclusion

Hopefully, this smoothie and juice recipe book has inspired you to whip up a few health-giving and delicious yourself, or even come up with your own special mixes. Making smoothies and juices is easy, fun and probably one of the single best things you can do for your health.

Thank you

Sara Banks

RELATED READING

I have the perfect complement to this e-book to further enhance your weight loss results. To truly lose weight and stay healthy long term you need to understand how your Leptin hormone is impacting your efforts to shed the weight and stay healthy long term.

I highly recommend that you check out my book "**Leptin Resistance Revealed**." It is now available on Amazon in both paperback and e-book formats.

ABOUT THE AUTHOR

I am an author, coach, and health and fitness enthusiast that loves to teach people about losing weight and feeling better about themselves. For many years I have been studying different diet techniques and approaches to transform the human body. One of my biggest passions is helping others achieve the body that they have always wanted. I receive great satisfaction from the success of other men and woman. I look forward to helping teach you how to be healthy and live a better life. Please check out my author page on Amazon to see my latest work.

Disclaimer

Please remember that anything discussed here does not constitute medical advice and cannot substitute for appropriate medical care.

Made in the USA
Columbia, SC
29 November 2019

84049085R00028

Duke Ellington:
A Life in Music

by Erick Montgomery

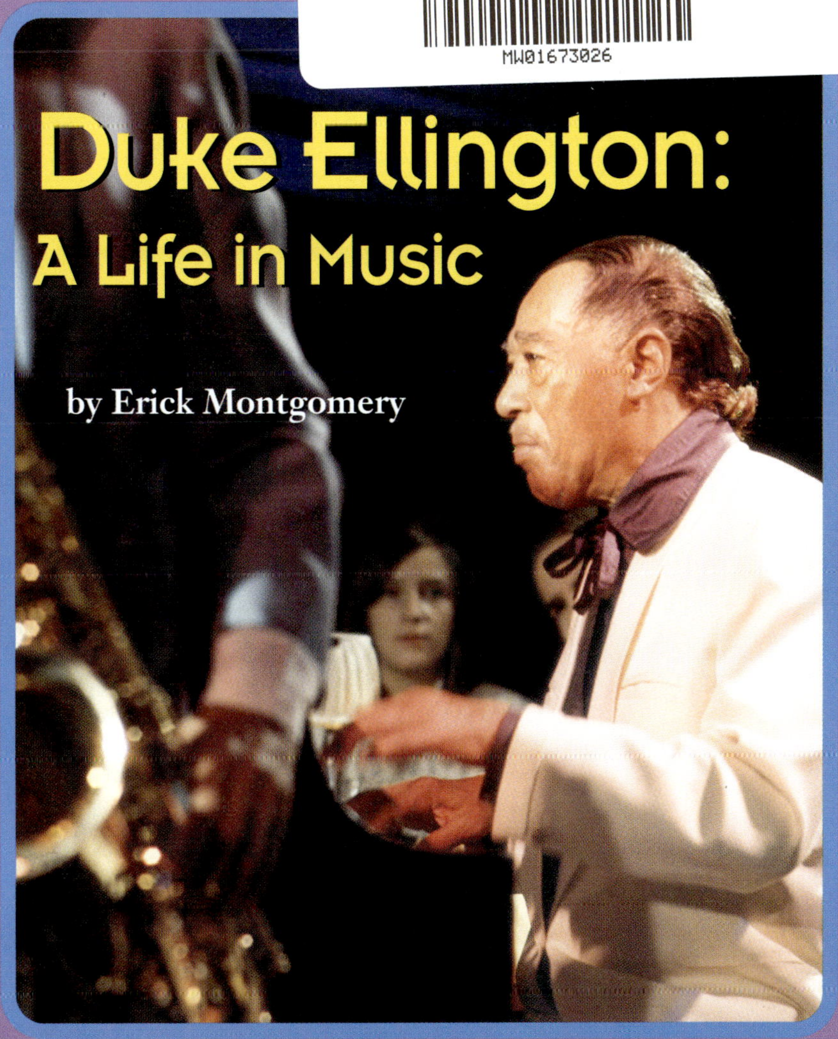

HOUGHTON MIFFLIN BOSTON

His real name was Edward, but his friends called him Duke. He was born in Washington, D.C., in 1899. His talent for music took him far from there. People all over the world came to know Duke Ellington. They knew him for his wonderful, new music and his beautiful smile.

Left: Duke Ellington at age four.

Top: The Duke Ellington Orchestra in 1927.

Duke was seven when he began to play the piano. He liked to play *ragtime* music. Ragtime was a lively music that sounded strong and fast. Playing ragtime gave Duke his quick fingers. It got him thinking of music all the time. At the age of fourteen he wrote his first song, "Soda Fountain Rag."

Duke began to earn money playing with bands all over Washington. Then, when he was 24, he went to New York City. That's where his music really took off.

In New York, Duke started his own band, the Duke Ellington Orchestra. An orchestra is a large band with many players playing many different instruments. Duke started his orchestra with twelve players.

By 1927, the Orchestra was playing at Harlem's famous Cotton Club. Duke played piano. He led the band. He also wrote the music. Duke had many big hits. The songs "Mood Indigo" and "Sophisticated Lady" were two of the first.

The Duke Ellington Orchestra also played live on the radio. That made it possible for people all over to hear Duke's music.

Duke was making a new kind of music. He had the players in his band *improvise* as they played. When musicians improvise, they make things up as they play. People were not used to such a bold sound. The Duke Ellington Orchestra became famous for their improvised music.

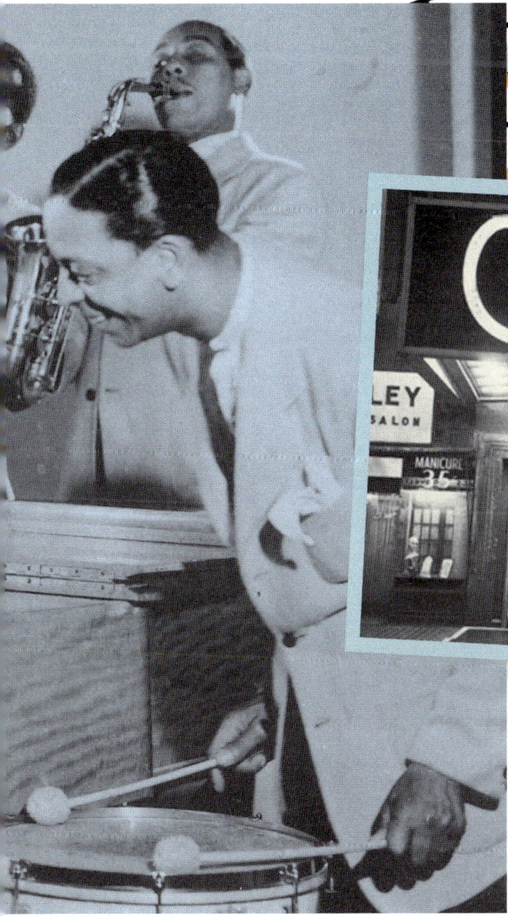

Top: The Cotton Club in Harlem, New York City.

Left: Duke and his improvising Orchestra.

Duke's Orchestra played a fun, fresh kind of music that people loved. It surprised people. It made them move. This music had smooth sounds that thrilled listeners. It had jumpy sounds too.

Duke Ellington writes a song with Billy Strayhorn.

Duke Ellington was at his best when great musicians worked with him. One of the greatest was a songwriter named Billy Strayhorn. When Duke met Billy, Duke knew he had found someone special. Billy became Duke's musical partner in 1939. Over the next forty years, they wrote hundreds of songs together. One was "Take the 'A' Train." It became the Duke Ellington Orchestra's best-known song.

In the 1930s and early 1940s, big bands like Duke's were playing a kind of music called *swing*. It was music to tap your feet to. It was music to get up and dance to. People made up new dances to go with the music. The Duke Ellington Orchestra performed swing music all over the United States.

All over America, people danced to swing music.

On January 23, 1943, the Duke Ellington Orchestra played in Carnegie Hall in New York City. Few African Americans had ever played at this beautiful, world-famous concert hall. Duke Ellington had *composed*, or made up, a new song for this special event.

Top: Duke performs at Carnegie Hall.

Right: Duke gets ready for Carnegie Hall.

Duke and his band played his song. It was called "Black, Brown, and Beige." This was not music to dance to. It was serious music for a big concert hall. Not everyone liked it. But Duke had always dreamed of making music that would tell the story of African Americans in a great way. With "Black, Brown, and Beige," Duke was making this dream come true.

Duke said that the music he wrote and played was "the voice of his people." And he took that music everywhere. It seemed that everyone who heard his music wanted to hear more and more.

Duke Ellington was famous for his energy. He never tired of writing music. When people asked him what his favorite song was, he liked to answer, "the next five coming up." He would keep writing songs for a long time to come.

Duke Ellington flashes his famous smile.

Duke's music was a bright light for U.S. soldiers in World War II.

From 1941 to 1945, the United States was fighting World War II. The Duke Ellington Orchestra helped to bring smiles to people's faces in a time of great sadness and worry. Soldiers could listen to his music and think about their families back home listening too. Duke's music was a bright light in a dark time.

Ella Fitzgerald sings a song.

It was not just the Duke Ellington Orchestra that people loved. People also wanted to hear the guest singers who sang with the Orchestra. Duke made sure that people got to hear the best. One singer was Ella Fitzgerald. Her singing was like no other. She used her voice as if it were an instrument.

Another famous player was Louis Armstrong. He was a gifted trumpet player. He sang too. His rough voice and his fantastic trumpet playing gave the Orchestra a New Orleans-style jazz sound. There was no one like Louis Armstrong, either!

Duke Ellington plays with Louis Armstrong.

President Richard Nixon presents Duke with the Presidential Medal of Freedom.

In 1969, Duke Ellington was given the Presidential Medal of Freedom. That honor is given to special people for service to the United States. Duke Ellington got his award for the years of beautiful music he had given to his country.

Duke Ellington was the most famous jazz musician of his time. Maybe of all time. He changed popular American music. Musicians all over copied him. He gave them the courage to try new ways of playing and singing music. Even today, young musicians study Duke's music. They dream of someday being as good as Duke was.

Today, musicians like Wynton Marsalis still play Duke's music.

Most people who met Duke Ellington were surprised by how gentle he was. That quiet, elegant man made people happy all over the world. For 50 years, he led the Duke Ellington Orchestra. He made the music that still makes people want to listen, tap their feet, and dance.